INFORMATION
EXPLORER
JUNIOR

Speak Out! Creating Podcasts and Other Audio Recordings

by Kristin Fontichiaro

CHERRY LAKE PUBLISHING · ANN ARBOR, MICHIGAN

A NOTE TO PARENTS AND TEACHERS: Please remind your children how to stay safe online before they do the activities in this book.

A NOTE TO KIDS: Always remember your safety comes first!

Published in the United States of America
by Cherry Lake Publishing
Ann Arbor, Michigan
www.cherrylakepublishing.com

Content Adviser: Gail Dickinson, PhD, Associate Professor, Old Dominion University, Norfolk, Virginia

Photo Credits: Cover, ©iStockphoto.com/omgimages; page 4, ©iStockphoto.com/zeremski; page 6, ©Fancy/Alamy; page 9 ©olly/Shutterstock, Inc.; page 15, ©iStockphoto.com/Graffizone; page 17, ©Dragon Images/Shutterstock, Inc.; page 21, ©IMS0033077/Media Bakery.

Library of Congress Cataloging-in-Publication Data
Fontichiaro, Kristin.
 Speak out! : creating podcasts and other audio recordings / by Kristin Fontichiaro.
  pages cm. — (Information explorer junior)
 Includes bibliographical references and index.
 ISBN 978-1-62431-022-5 (lib. bdg.) — ISBN 978-1-62431-046-1 (pbk.) — ISBN (e-book) 978-1-62431-070-6 (e-book)
 1. Podcasting—Juvenile literature. I. Title.
 TK5105.887.F647 2013
 006.7'876—dc23   2012035764

Cherry Lake Publishing would like to acknowledge the work of The Partnership for 21st Century Skills. Please visit www.21stcenturyskills.org for more information.

Printed in the United States of America
Corporate Graphics Inc.
January 2013
CLSP12

Table of Contents

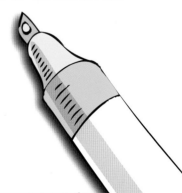

CHAPTER ONE

What Is Podcasting?

The last time you listened to something online or on the radio, did it make you want your own show? Do you like asking people questions? Is it fun to act things out or share

You can listen to shows, music, or other recordings online.

Podcasts can be transferred to MP3 players to listen to on the go.

information? Then sharing **audio** recordings may be for you!

A podcast is an audio recording you make and share. You can use your voice or musical instruments. You can also add music files and sound effects. These make your recording come alive. When you finish your recording, you can share it online. You can also e-mail it. You could even **transfer** it to an MP3 player.

Maybe you could record a song with friends or family.

People make many kinds of recordings. They might ask trivia questions. Some people do a game play-by-play. Others interview people. Peter likes to record guitar solos. Maria acts out stories. Journalists use podcasts to share up-to-date news stories. If you can record it and share it online, it's a podcast!

To make a podcast, you will need:

- a computer, tablet, or smartphone
- an Internet connection
- podcasting software or an app (turn to page 23 for ideas)
- a **microphone** (one might be built into your device)
- a Web site where you can post your podcast
- an adult's permission

Your librarian or teacher may have supplies you can use.

Ask a parent, teacher, or librarian for help if you need it.

7

Activity

To get ideas for recordings, try listening to several radio stations. What kinds of conversations and **commercials** do you hear? Which do you remember? List things that grab your attention. These ideas can help make your recordings exciting.

Listen for:

- music
- sound effects
- voices (such as accents, different ages and genders, and funny voices)
- word choice
- humor
- emotion

CHAPTER TWO

Planning

Before recording, you should have a plan. You can start with something short and easy. Have you ever heard someone selling something on the radio? That was a commercial. A short, 15- or 30-second **advertisement** (or ad) is a great first recording!

A good ad makes you believe that a product is worth buying. Does this photograph convince you to buy this person's product?

An ad could sell a service, such as babysitting.

Think about what you want to sell. Ads can sell a product, such as toothpaste or granola bars. Ads can sell a service. Lawn mowing and babysitting are services. Some ads sell an experience. This can be a movie or concert. **Trailers** are ads for books, movies, or TV shows.

You could also **persuade** people to take action. You might want people to protect the environment or stay healthy. These commercials are called public service announcements, or PSAs.

There are many ways to make an ad. One simple plan is:

1 **Start with a hook**. A hook is an exciting sentence that grabs the listener's attention. For example, "Did you know that YOU can save the planet?"

2 **Explain why people should do what you suggest**. For example, "Recycle instead of throwing things away. Recycled homework papers are made into new paper. Recycled bottles can be turned into new bottles or even fleece!"

3 **Wrap it up with a memorable sentence**. For example, "So do your share—let's recycle!"

Let's try making a podcast movie trailer. Start by organizing your ideas. You're going to need three sections for your trailer. Here is an example for the movie *The Wizard of Oz*.

HOOK: Have you ever wanted to escape to another world?

EXPLAIN: Dorothy did! A tornado swoops her off to the Land of Oz. In Oz, lions talk and monkeys fly! But watch out! The Wicked Witch of the West wants Dorothy's ruby slippers.

WRAP UP: Will Dorothy and her friends make it to the Wizard? Will the Wizard grant their wishes and get Dorothy home? Or will the Wicked Witch of the West get to Dorothy first? Watch *The Wizard of Oz* to find out!

When you have all three parts written down, you have a **script**! Practice saying your script out loud.

You need to speak clearly and carefully in your recording. Repeat it until you feel comfortable saying the words. Then you are ready to record.

Activity

Think of your favorite movie or book. Write a script. Then trade with a partner. What can you do to make each other's ideas even better?

To get a copy of this activity, visit www.cherrylakepublishing.com/activities.

CHAPTER THREE

Recording

Set up your equipment in a quiet place. Go to page 7 for a full list of what you need Review your software's buttons or **icons**. How do you start and stop recording? When you are ready,

- take a deep breath;
- press the Record button;
- speak clearly and slowly;
- press Stop when you are done.

You did it! Play back your recording. Your voice might sound different than it does inside your head. That's normal. If you like what you recorded, save it. If not, delete it and record it again.

14

To get a copy of this activity, visit www.cherrylakepublishing.com/activities.

Activity

You can use different kinds of voices in your recording. Can your voice go really high? What about low? Try making your voice sound scary or funny. Can you use an accent? See what you can do!

How can you make your voice sound different?

CHAPTER FOUR

Adding Music or Sound Effects

A podcast with your voice is great. Adding music or sound effects is even better! Music sets the mood of a recording. It can make your recording happy, sad, or scary. Sound effects help listeners imagine things they can't see. For example, Maria wants her listeners to picture a school. She adds the sound of a bell ringing. When a character breaks a window, Maria adds the sound of breaking glass.

What do you think of when you hear a bell?

You can find music and sound effects online. (Look at page 23 for ideas.) Remember, you need permission to use other people's recordings. But it's also a lot of fun to make your own!

Ask for help if you're not sure whether you can use a recording you find online.

Activity

What music or sound effects would make these podcasts even better?

1. An interview with your principal
2. A play that takes place on a busy city street
3. A nature program set in the woods
4. A commercial inviting people to visit your town

BEEP!
BEEP!

To get a copy of this activity, visit www.cherrylakepublishing.com/activities.

CHAPTER FIVE

Editing, Exporting, Sharing

It is important to review your recording. Make sure it sounds just right. You might find things you want to change or fix. This is called editing. Here are some questions to think about:

- **Am I too quiet?** If so, move your mouth closer to the microphone. Some podcasting software will help you make your voice louder.

- **Do I have dead air?** Radio announcers call moments of unwanted silence "dead air." There could be dead air at the beginning or end of your recording. Dead air might also happen when you pause. Cut those empty spots. You'll sound more like an expert!

- **Do my words make sense?** It's always fine to record again if you get a new, better idea.

  After editing, you are ready to **export** your recording. This turns it into an Internet-friendly format. Follow your software or app's instructions.

  Your podcast is now ready for an audience. Time to share it! You can e-mail it to friends or family, or post it to your class's **wiki** or Web page. You can also burn it to a CD or load it onto an MP3 player. Ask an adult for help.

  Congratulations, podcaster! You've learned a fun and creative way to show what you know.

Stay Safe Online!
1. Ask an adult for permission before you publish anything.
2. Keep your private information private. Do not include your last name, address, school, or teacher's name in your podcast.

To get a copy of this activity, visit www.cherrylakepublishing.com/activities.

Activity

Listen to your trailer. Could you add or change the music and sounds? Is there dead air? Take some time to edit and revise your work. When everything sounds just the way you want it, export the files following your software's instructions.

Make sure your trailer sounds just the way you want it to sound.

Glossary

advertisement (ad-vur-TIZE-muhnt) a broadcast or published notice that calls attention to something

audio (AW-dee-oh) having to do with how sound is heard, recorded, and played back

commercials (kuh-MUR-shuhlz) audio or video advertisements

export (EK-sport) to create a copy of a computer file in a different format so it can be used with another program

icons (EYE-kahnz) graphic symbols on the desktop of a computer screen representing programs, functions, or files

microphone (MYE-kruh-fone) an instrument that is used to record sound or make sound louder

persuade (pur-SWADE) to convince someone to do or believe something by giving the person good reasons

script (SKRIPT) the written text of a play, movie, television show, radio show, or commercial

trailers (TRAY-lurz) commercials for a book, movie, or television show

transfer (TRANTS-fer) to move a file from one computer or device to another

wiki (WIH-kee) a Web site that allows many users to add and change information

Find Out More

BOOKS

Fontichiaro, Kristin. *Podcasting 101*. Ann Arbor, MI: Cherry Lake, 2010.

Sawyer, Sarah. *Career Building Through Podcasting*. New York: Rosen, 2008.

Sturm, Jeanne. *MP3 Players*. Vero Beach, FL: Rourke Publishing, 2009.

WEB SITES

Audacity

http://audacity.sourceforge.net

Ask an adult for permission and help with downloading this free software. It will help you with recording and editing. You'll also find instructions for downloading the free LAME converter. This program is needed to export your podcasts in MP3 format for publishing.

Creative Commons Search

http://search.creativecommons.org

When people add a Creative Commons license to their work, that gives you permission to use it in your own projects. Use this site to find great music and sound effects for your podcast!

Index

About the Author

Kristin Fontichiaro teaches at the University of Michigan. Her students make podcasts for class.